Reflections at Sundown

Looking back at what really mattered

Revised 3/2010

Reflections at Sundown

Looking back at what really mattered

Inge Etzbach

Reflections at Sundown

Looking back at what really mattered

Revised 3/2010

Etzbach, Inge, 1932-

Reflections at Sundown
Looking back at what really mattered
ISBN: 1450520502
EAN-13: 9781450520508

Printed in the United States of America

Almvillabooks

Website: almvillabooks.net
e-mail: almvillabooks@gmail.com

$12.95

Dedicated

to my friend George, a gentle warrior whose aim
was always to be the best he could be,

and

to Anna Baltzer who has courage and clarity
of vision and stood up when her name was
called

Contents

Reflections at Sundown 1

The War Years 4

A German Girl in Uniform.......................... ...13

Kibbutz Eilon in Israel................................. 20

Serving under the Israeli Flag................ 27

Who am I? Discovering My Jewish Roots............ 33

Travelling through Israel/Palestine.................. 39

Hebron...44

Mt. Sinai 50

Jerusalem...53

Trying to find answers 57

Looking back at what really mattered 62

Biography

Reference

Reflections at Sundown

I am 77 years old and well aware that my time is limited. During the day I walk and talk and do as if there is an endless line of tomorrows waiting for me, but in the evening I sit on the deck and watch the sun go down. The formation of clouds glides by in glowing red and pink, reminding me to hurry and wrap up my life and state – for myself – once and for all what I consider "the Truth" worthy of living and exploring and accepting. What did I learn? Facts, many facts, many superficial, pointless, needless facts. I nursed false hopes, took wrong turns, followed unsuitable examples, neglected prudent advice, and got confused, made concessions. There is also proof, over and over again, that human nature basically does not change despite attempts at reason and compassion. Greed and unthinking cruelty still are inflicted on others, be it on other nations, families, races, human beings, animals and the environment. Now I need to sort out the insights which are worth keeping among these many details of my life, and hold them close to me when the sun goes down and the glowing sky turns dark.

I had good parent who cared for me and my two sisters. I had a loving husband and three good and decent children, whom we cared for in turn and helped find a place in life. But the focal point of my interest and preoccupation for many years was the desire to come to terms with the major global conflicts through which I lived: the War in Germany with air raids, insecurity, death and loss of God and faith; my years as a member in the Hitler Youth embedded entirely in the Nazi worldview, the reality of the Holocaust right in front of my eyes; my stint as a volunteer in a Kibbutz and in the Israeli Army, and finally my travel in the Middle East and the recognition of the Israeli/Palestinian conflict, which generated deep compassion not only for the Israelis, but for the Palestinians as well. The most important thing, for me, is the conviction that the destruction of one people by another must never happen again to Jews or to people of any other religious, racial, ethnic or national origin.

Philosophy is an attempt to come to terms with Death, I read once. At the age of 44 I entered College to study Philosophy and Political Science and the meaning of death and life and words and paradigms and ethics and what is eternal and what is fleeting, and how one knows the difference. This led to some time spent at the Truman Institute for the Advancement of Peace at Hebrew University in Jerusalem, a place in which to see the world through many different contemporary eyes.

Now I live in a small town in upstate New York, surrounded by hills and trees and a wide sky, nursing a benign growing brain tumor that causes headaches and may become the thing which will put an end to my life. But please, not before I have a chance to take stock! I need to think and weigh and decide what was important and what is worthy and worth saving in ideas and facts and experiences, in decisions and values and ethical choices. Those mark my long path as a human being in search of an answer.

The War Years

The other day somebody said that I was too involved in the memory of the War. She was visibly annoyed and said that every example I give about anything human goes back to something that happened to me during the war, and she for her part would like to forget it and go on with life. Perhaps she is right. It is just that I can't forget it. It is the one thing that my entire identity is built up around. My feeling about death, my doubt of the existence of God, my conviction of the meaningless of life and the underlying sense of hopeless-ness, my search for a better answer and an ethical way to live – all go back to the War. If one would take the War away from me, I think I would not be the same person.

It was going badly – everybody knew, but nobody mentioned it. Everybody was afraid to speak the truth because that could land you in jail (for injuring the fighting spirit of the population). For several years, Germany, in its inexplicable hubris and arrogance, had flooded Europe: from the top of Norway to Greece, the Balkans and North Africa and of course Russia. Now, in the middle of a bitter winter came demands to collect gloves and socks for the suffering troops. There were notices of the deaths of fathers, sons and uncles in the wide expanse of a snow-covered foreign land. In the icy hell of Russia even the souls of the survivors froze and broke under the impact of destruction, fear, hunger and thirst, icy cold and stark hopelessness. 5.5 million German soldiers died during the war; 8.5 million Russian soldiers did not survive. Those who came home carried the wounds until they died.

The "home front" suffered under unending air raids. Saturation bombings caused the death of hundreds of thousands of German civilians. The people, in the midst of this destruction, plodded on, not knowing what else to do. We lived in a bubble of misery and had no strength to even consider the misery of people in jails or concentration camps.

Food was scarce and we were hungry all the time. One day I took a train with my aunt to a small town near the North Sea where we walked from farmhouse to farmhouse, trying to get an egg or a piece of sausage in exchange for postcards, coat hangers and little bags of tea which my aunt had repackaged. The train both ways was hopelessly overcrowded with people on the roof and hanging out of windows. I climbed in through the toilet window, half in and half out of the small smelly cubicle. That's where I, only 10 years old, clung to the window frame for 5 hours while others, men and women, used the toilet (if they were lucky enough to fight their way in). My aunt stood on the platform between carriages. Bombers flew overhead, but we were not allowed to leave the train and were frozen in sheer fright.

I knew of three different kinds of bombs. There were the regular combustion bombs which were not announced by any noise, but just hit a building or the ground and exploded with a deafening crash, causing a deep crater and destroying everything in sight. Then there were air mines. They had a weight of up to several tons, had a thin outer skin and exploded either in the air above the target. They caused a tremendous pressure wave flattening a large area, reducing it to rubble and giving incendiary bombs access to do their job, or utilized a trigger mechanism detonating the bomb at ground level. Air mines approached with a very distinctive whistling noise. You could hear the high whine coming closer and closer, then hit the target and explode, while the next whine came closer. The city of Hamburg was bombed in "Operation Gomorrah" by British and American planes around the clock for eight days and seven nights. A firestorm of 1500 degrees Fahrenheit resulted, burnt and suffocated 50,000 people in one night alone and destroyed 250,000 houses. Refugees from the surrounding areas arrived in my hometown, shell-shocked and half-crazed. I remember the white faces and blank eyes of the children.

Then there were phosphor bombs which – I was told – were sticks filled with a gel-like liquid which exploded and burst into flames. The gel stuck to the skin and fire flared up whenever oxygen came in contact with it. Wuppertal, a neighboring small town in a narrow valley with houses climbing up the wooded hills on both side of the river Wupper, had already suffered many bombing raids before. The one in May 1943 caused 3,500 dead, and that one employed phosphor bombs. There were horror stories over the next few days about people burning like torches, jumping into the river Wupper to extinguish the flames. As soon as they tried to climb back on land, the phosphor caused the fire to flare up again. The next attack in June 1943 killed over 2,500 people in one night. Statistics for the small town of Wuppertal show that

- 12,000 soldiers and 7,000 civilians from Wuppertal were killed during the war

- 6,500 soldiers and 327 civilians disappeared without a trace
- sirens announced approaching bomber squadrons 2,700 times – mostly at night – forcing inhabitants to flee into the cellars and air raid shelters
- 638,000 bombs and 300,000 phosphor bombs were dropped on Wuppertal.

I cannot help comparing 9/11, horrible as it was, with only one of these air raids on even one of these towns.

May 31, 1943 was my mother's birthday and the day started peacefully. My mother gave us the one slice of bread with rendered pig lard and salt (which was all there was for breakfast) and I went to school with my sister. By 9 a.m. the sirens were howling in pre-warning mode (meaning the danger was not yet acute), but the school closed anyway and we ran home and sat in the cellar until the bombers (on their way to some larger city) had passed overhead and the end alarm was given. We walked back to school. The Girl's High School had been destroyed in a bombing raid, so we had to walk 10 minutes farther to the Boy's High School which had given us permission to have our classes in a former storeroom. By 12 PM there was another alarm. Again we ran home. My mother gave us some cabbage stew (without meat, meat was only available on coupons and consisted of a small piece every two weeks) and we were in the cellar until 3 pm. It is a wonder that there was any learning at all, especially considering the fact that there were no books whatsoever, not even paper to write on.

Another alarm sounded for the returning bombers at 5 pm, and again, we spent 2 hours in the cellar with airplanes droning overhead. My father had outfitted the cellar with steel doors and sandbags around window openings and also some bunk beds so that we children could sleep there. At 7 pm my mother handed out bowls with some more cabbage and the second slice of bread with pig lard for dinner, before we went to sleep on the straw-filled sack mattresses.

But this was the night for a major raid on our town. The preliminary and acute alarms sounded one after the other, so loud it almost caused the heart to stop. Bombs exploded in the neighborhood with crashes that deafened the ears. The factories near the railroad station and the surrounding neighborhoods were targeted. Then came the high-pitched whine of an air mine, and the deafening sound of it slamming into a house down the street. I remember the floor of the cellar rising like a wave, pushing my knees into my chin. The air was filled with choking clouds of dust flaking from the shaking walls. Fear was so thick that you could taste it. And then the next high-pitched whine came closer, louder and louder, and I, a child of 10, KNEW that it would hit us and our lives would end in the next second, crushed under rubble, like all the other thousands of victims in this rotten war. I said good-bye to the world and waited like a mute, resigned animal for death. But the air mine kept whistling and passed over us and slammed into a house on the other side, killing all its inhabitants, and in choking clouds of dust I realized that I was still alive and that death had passed me by.

I came out of that cellar the next day a changed person. I had tasted death, and life would never look the same. My family survived; the people in the houses hit by the two bombs had been killed. My girlfriend was one of them. Why? Why her and not me? Where was the reason in this? Where was God? How can you ever believe that your actions count, that there is meaning to life if this vast, impersonal power may come out of nowhere and wipe you off the table, regardless of your merit, regardless of the goodness of your soul, regardless of anything you want or do or aspire to? My girlfriend's parents were good, decent people. Why them, and why the two younger sisters who were still babies?

The search for meaning in the face of such an impersonal, cruel, senseless universe, has been occupying me ever since. Life and death, justice and indifference, goodness and egotism, compassion and cruelty – these questions haunt me daily and demand answers in an empty world in which, I believe, God himself died of a broken heart.

Sometimes, in the past, I used to wish that there was a God whom I could ask for help, one I could hold on to, who would look after me, who would give meaning to my life. It is hard to feel so isolated in an empty universe. I remember once I flew across the continent and the plane got into a tremendous storm which buffeted it, lifted it up and repeatedly dropped it. It was frightening beyond words. I, the agnostic, held onto the armrest and prayed "Please God, help!" But when the incident was over, I was still the old agnostic, the doubter, convinced that while there may be a God who put the laws in motion, there was no God who looked after each and every one of us. If there really was a God who looked after man, why did he not look after the 30 million people who died during the last war, and the 6 million suffering and dying during the holocaust?

Faith in the conventional sense is very difficult for me — I cannot muster faith. As an agnostic, I have more questions than answers. The following saying by Rev. Forrest Church comes closest to what I believe:

The power which I cannot explain or know or name I call God. God is my name for the mystery that looms within and arches beyond the limits of my being. Life force, spirit of life, ground of being; these too are names for the unnamable which I am now content to call

My God.

The Girl in Uniform

The picture shows me as a young girl in pigtails and uniform shirt, looking unflinchingly into the camera. No coyness here, no flirting glance, no smiling attempt to be pleasant or funny or pretty. You are what you are – and proud of your substance, not trying to improve your form. The eyes look straight at you; the mouth is set firmly and shows strength. To be German meant to be straight-forward, truthful, without deceit, healthy, dependable, honest, obedient. It meant the willingness to work without whining and excuses and to be proud of the history of our country and conscious of our part in its future. Life was serious and needed to be approached as such.

The national and political environment under the Nazis had the aim of transforming the people into a dedicated part of the political system. Looking at the picture I can see some of the results, but in my mind I see what went on underneath the surface. As in the United States with its pledge of allegiance which children are drilled to deliver every morning, we had our own rituals. For example, we were required to chant slogans in unison at times, such as: "I am nothing – my people are everything!" or "Fuehrer, command us – we will obey you!" We also firmly believed that our country was the best and most enlightened country in the world, (so we were told).

Membership in the Hitler Youth was mandatory from the age of 10 and from then on we had not only civic lessons in school, but also twice-weekly Youth group meetings heavily laced with Nazi propaganda. I became a leader of a small group of girls after a few years and participated, like everybody else, in teaching, camping, marching and sports, all activities, which were, in part, somewhat like what girl scouts do in other countries. However, parades, speeches, uniforms, adulation of Hitler, were woven into the experiences of my childhood. But there was no mention of the right to personal opinion or the right to one's own conviction. That was not part of the fascist worldview. Control of the press meant of course that no dissenting voices and opinions were heard and only the Nazi viewpoint was presented. If you spoke up you could land in jail. Members of the Hitler Youth were even reminded to report on their parents if they spoke against the Party!

My grandmother, who ran a bar, had been known to be a Communist sympathizer before the Nazi takeover. In order to show that she had reformed her ways, she subscribed to a violently anti-semitic paper called "Der Stuermer", exclusively devoted to the vilification and degradation of Jews. Several times a week I visited my grandmother and, while she served me a glass of lemonade, I read "Der Stuermer". I learned to read by studying "Der Stuermer". As a result I, 6-7-8 years old, took in the most extreme Nazi views together with my lemonade. If you had asked me then, I would have cheerfully stated that: there are people who deserve to live and others who are better off dead; that it is perfectly acceptable to cleanse the world of "scum"; that there should be no compassion for sub-humans; and that the safety and security of the German nation justified extreme measures (something like preemptive strikes). I, who had never met a Jew in person, hated all Jews with a vengeance. And I hated and despised with the same intensity Russians, Poles, blacks, retarded people, handicapped people - inferior or worthless life, as it was called. This is what indoctrination is – it constitutes the sea in which a human being swims and learns.

In 1945 we moved to a little village to escape the interminable bombing raids. One morning armed American soldiers occupied the village. They proceeded down the road and discovered a work camp filled with half-starved, sick, emaciated men in striped prison uniforms whose only desire was to get away from this place of horror. The afternoon I was standing at the front door, shaking, crying, looking at the endless stream of pitiful humanity, of men hardly able to walk yet supporting others even sicker - dehumanized men who still had the compassion to care about others. What I had considered inferior and worthless life before, I saw now as suffering, broken-down human beings capable of more decency and kindness than anybody I had known before. The awful realization rose up in me, gripping my heart and my soul and my mind, that the Truth I had been told to believe had instead been a horrible Lie, that we all had been duped, deceived and misled. I was overwhelmed by the growing conviction that my compliance made me responsible for the suffering and death of countless humans, and that I had unknowingly participated in man's inhumanity to man.

That afternoon I stood at the front door and swore that I would never, ever believe anything anybody told me without checking it out first, that I would never, ever follow any doctrine, political or religious, without making sure that it was based on Truth, and that I would never, ever follow any man without the most critical analysis of his character and message. While my friends proceeded into their teenage years concerned with dances and boys, I was obsessed with atoning for my guilt concerning the horrors perpetrated by me by virtue of association.

For many years I carried the burden of the Holocaust, it seems, on my shoulders. Every time I met a person whose family had died in the camps, who himself had suffered dislocation and cruelty at the hands of my people, I bled inside. When I was in my 50's I visited Israel and Palestine and had an experience that lifted this particular burden off my soul. I was sitting at a café in the Old City of Jerusalem and overheard a group of Israelis and Americans, obviously Jews, at the next table speak about Arabs. One of them said: "One should line them all up against the wall and mow them down with submachine guns!" I sat there, ice cold and shaken, and finally got up, went over to their table, identified myself as German and pointed out that my people had actually done to Jews what they were proposing to do to Arabs, and did they really mean it? There was a deep silence, and finally one of them apologized and said he had not been thinking and he was sorry. Others said the same thing – I felt they meant it. It was then that I realized that evil lurks in the human souls of all people of all nations and religions, and I was finally able to let go of the idea of a specific, unshakeable German character flaw. That burden was replaced by the knowledge of sharing in a larger, more universal truth, namely a responsibility for all humanity.

What did I learn from this? First of all, that every human being has inherent worth and dignity. Neither race nor ethnicity nor class bestows value on one over the other. If there is ever an example of the need for ethics in dealing with our fellow human beings, it is the holocaust. Even just the thought of the horror of this time proves the absolute need for a conscience, for kindness and compassion.

As much as I suffered from the knowledge of what my people had done to others, I also realized that we cannot undo the past, and it is not enough to just bemoan the past. I believe that it is up to all of us to make sure that the horrors exemplified by the Holocaust will never again happen to people of any religious, racial, ethnic or national origin. After all, we are our brother's keeper.

When I first reflected on this time of my life, I firmly believed that it is individuals - individuals with a conscience, with kindness and compassion in their hearts, determined to heal and not to hurt - who make the difference when darkness threatens. I believed then that a country full of individuals with a conscience might even be able to prevent darkness. I still hold onto this belief, but also know that personal ethics are sometimes overpowered by the purposes and goals of tribes, nations and other groups.

Kibbutz Eilon in Galilee

My husband, only 54 years old, died in 1987. I had been his constant care giver for months, and his death, even though expected, devastated me. It brought out all these memories about existence and death and insecurity which had been a companion throughout my youth. After a month I went back to work, but sank deeper and deeper into a dark, black hole and finally decided I needed to get away, far away to a country where I had never been and where nothing reminded me of home. And that was when the possibility of going to Israel arose. My heart drew me there, but Israel also offered the opportunity to work as a volunteer for room and board, and that would make a longer stay possible.

32 years was the cut-off point for volunteers, I learned, and I would not qualify. But a friend had an uncle in a Kibbutz in Israel's North who was willing to make arrangements for "Rose's friend from New York" so that I could come to his

Kibbutz and join the volunteers from other countries working in kitchen, laundry, stables and fields. This is how I arrived one day in January at the gates of the Kibbutz: a 54 year old sad lady with a backpack, who badly needed a new direction.

Eilon is a lovely place, nestled on the side of the Lebanon mountain range. The weather is mild. Flowers are blooming year round. A sweet smell of orange blossoms fills the air. The residents live in small apartments or houses, meals are eaten in the communal dining hall, everybody's laundry is done centrally, and everybody has a job and works in the area most suited to his or her talents. The General Membership Meetings discuss and vote on all issues. Eilon is like many other communal settlements, but it is different in one way: the children, who used to live and be reared in children's houses, now lived with their parents, are picked up by them after work, and spend their evenings at home.

I went to the Volunteer Office and met some very friendly and welcoming people. I had come to work as a volunteer and did not think that they expected "Rose's Jewish friend from New York". When I handed over my German pass-port, I noticed that all 3 ladies in the room paled noticeably and were very upset – it seemed that the Kibbutz had been founded by Concentration Camp survivors who had decided unanimously at its founding that no German volunteers would be admitted. I was asked why I did not become an American citizen before? After all, I had been in the United States for 30 years already. I explained that I had not wanted to give up my German citizenship because to me it meant to give up my guilt and responsibility – as I saw it – for the Holocaust. Becoming a US citizen would have wiped the slate clean, and I did not want that. And what about my father? "What did he do during Hitler's time?" they asked. I did not think that I should be responsible for my father's convictions or actions, whatever they were. I wanted to be looked at as a person responsible for my own ethical choices. After all, I was only 12 years old at the end of the war – why should I be blamed for something which happened before I was able to choose sides?

It was a very disturbing 15 minutes in which I had to explain myself, my family, my worldview. Finally I offered to leave, took my backpack and walked to the door. I suppose they looked at this old lady who had come clear across the globe to work for them without pay, and they felt sorry for me. So I was invited to stay and work in the kitchen, and a small apartment was assigned to my use.

It was a lonely string of months in Eilon, but a welcoming, healing time, too. The Kibbutz had about 700 members, so preparation for mealtimes was long and monotonous. The volunteers were all much younger, from different countries, and could not relate to me much. Rose's relatives, however, were nice and often invited me to Friday's evening meals. Dov, the patriarch of the family, had long discussions with me about the history of Palestine and his life as a boy in Roumania, and he also told me that many Labour Party members had hoped for a state for all inhabitants of the region, Jewish and Arab alike, and were disappointed in the development of a specifically Jewish State. At one point I spent 3 days at the headquarters of the Kibbutz Organization in Givat Haviva and studied the development of the Kibbutz system because I planned to make that the topic of my master's thesis.

Otherwise I did not have much close contact with other inhabitants. Life was very much oriented towards families and children, and in general the residents did not encourage contact with volunteers - because volunteers come and go and any established connection is bound to end sooner or later. I did some travelling on the Sabbath. Once I joined up with another volunteer, and we rented a car and drove to Safad, a town in the highlands near Lake Kinneret. Safad, an old established Jewish Orthodox town, had an artist colony and many exhibits in utterly charming old houses up and down the hills. The Golan Heights, formerly part of Syria, reach down to the Eastern shore of the Lake, and on the Northern side are the ruins of an old synagogue and of Christian buildings which attract many Christian pilgrims. We took a boat across the lake – the sunlight on the lake is magical - and were silent in that place where Jesus is reported to have walked on the water. Not too far from there we drove past the Horns of Hittin, the two humps of hills where the last fight between the Crusaders and the Saracens took place in 1187: the crusaders wearing their iron chainmail, defending the top of the hill, and the Saracens stacking and burning wood all around, roasting the crusaders in their iron suits and thereby winning the battle. This country is so full of history involving Jews, Christians and Muslims alike. I can't help but be fascinated by the place.

Sometimes we went on bus tours. The one tour which still stays in my mind was to a demonstration by Peace Now, the non-governmental organization closely in sympathy with the Kibbutz System. It promoted the need and possibility for achieving a just peace and conciliation with the Palestinian people and neighboring Arab countries. We kitchen workers prepared a picnic lunch and loaded everything into the bus for a trip to Israel's King's Square in Tel Aviv.

The huge square was jammed with people in high spirits. The first intifada which had started a few months earlier was considered by Peace Now a political act; therefore the movement called for negotiations with the Palestinians, aimed at ending the occupation of the West Bank and Gaza and promoting a just peace between the two peoples. The speeches were received with great enthusiasm, the crowds clapped and danced and listened to singers, who expressed their peaceful spirit through songs. And finally, the band played the Israeli national anthem. The soulful strains of the song filled the air; everybody stood still and joined in song. Many people had tears in their eyes and there was not one person among the crowd of 100,000 who was not filled with the love and hope for their country Israel. I was very touched to see the descendents of Jews who had suffered through pogroms during many centuries of Diaspora, and finally through the cataclysmic hate of the holocaust, celebrate the existence of their own state - which finally belonged to them and gave them a home. Many of the people around me had been in concentration camps. The tattooed numbers on their wrists marked them forever, and their memories tortured them still.

I stood, deeply shaken, filled with love for these people, and listened to the huge crowd sing the national anthem. I knew that I would never forget the need and desire and right of these people to have a homeland of their own, to occupy this sliver of land in the very place where their forefathers lived centuries ago.

On this very square, during another Peace Now rally in November of 1995, Yitzhak Rabin, the Prime Minister of Israel, was killed by a right-wing student - not by a stranger or a neighboring Arab, but by one of Israel's own Jews. This wound has never been healed and has grave repercussions for the peaceful solution of the desperate struggle in the Middle East.

When I left Kibbutz Eilon after several months, I said good-bye to the volunteer office ladies and was told that, on the preceding evening, the General Membership had voted unanimously from then on to admit German volunteers "because we have to start building bridges".

I love these people. They went through hell and despair, and preserved or developed in their hearts a purity of sentiment I would like to bottle and distribute all over the world.

Serving under the Flag of Israel

I could not really believe it myself – but here I was, a "Volunteer for Israel", serving in the maintenance division of a tank battalion stationed at the Jordanian border. We were six middle-aged women from all over the United States, all Jewish except me, living together in a broken-down barracks room on a broken-down desolate scrap of an army base between Jerusalem and Tel Aviv. The flag pole in the center of the base was where we all congregated in the morning to be present at the raising of the Israeli flag.

We were each issued a uniform (a typical set of green Israeli fatigues making no attempt at fit or proper size) and a pair of army-issue lace-up boots. The get-up had a very interesting effect: we would walk across the assembly space between the various buildings and the mess hall and work sheds, with our hands up to our elbows in the cargo pockets of the pants – and our gait, our posture, our entire behavior would turn us into a very crude picture of male warriors. We all would immediately forget our "ladyness" and would curse like merce-naries. Our work freed Israeli soldiers to devote their time to the defense of the Israeli homeland. Three different kinds of jobs were to be performed by us: periodically climb all over army trucks to unhook and test, charge and re-install truck batteries, unpack hundreds of duffle bags with uniforms and gear to make sure that no mice had gotten in, and carefully pack everything up again according to size, and clean and oil Uzi guns. All of these jobs were very important. If war should break out in the middle of the night, thousands of reservists would descend on the base, grab a duffle bag and an Uzi off a rack, jump on a truck and drive to the border. All pieces of equipment had to be in perfect working order.

My job was cleaning and oiling Uzi guns. I would stand there in my army fatigues, grab the gun, stand it upright on the workbench, pull down the lever – bang, bang, bang – remove the cartridge, submerge the entire gun in a barrel with cleaning fluid (no gloves, no protection against the toxic fluid) then dunk the gun into a barrel with oil and finally stand it on a rack under which the ground was soaked with the run-off oil. Hour after hour, day after day. In my mind's eye were the lines of soldiers depending on my work in their duty to defend Israel. I was, at that time, still caught in my painful knowledge of the suffering of the Jews at the hands of my people. It gave me comfort to know that I could work to help give them a homeland and a place in the world where the word Jew was not a curse word, but one of pride.

We would eat together with the soldiers. That's where I learned the fact that Jews are not just Jews. They are from two main cultural groups serving in the same army together as citizens of the same country, but tending to congregate to others of their own group: Ashkenazim (from Europe) and Sephardim (originally from Spain, who spread to Muslim Countries in North Africa, Yemen etc. after the Inquisition). Some of the officers looked quite Arabic, dark and Middle-Eastern, and spoke Arabic among them-selves to my perpetual amazement. I made friends with some of the young Jewish female soldiers who were doing their year of national service. They gave me some insight into the mindset of Israeli-born Jews, so-called Sabras (from the native fruit which is prickly on the outside and sweet on the inside) and their fiancés in other units. This is another split in the Israeli population: the Sabras full of self-confidence in the accomplishments of their country, unwilling to ever again march to the gas chambers without fighting back, and the holocaust survivors, with their burden of experience gained in another time and place.

Passover and Easter fell together during that year, and we had 4 days to ourselves. I decided to jump on an army truck on its way to Jerusalem, sitting between soldiers and their guns, holding on to my back pack and feeling as free as never before in my life. Here I was, 54 years old, and free like a bird. My three children in New York did not know where I was and could not reach me, even if they wanted to. The truck left me off at Jaffa Gate at the Old City of Jerusalem – sending shivers down my spine – right next to the City of David! I climbed off the truck and walked down the small alley called King David Road, marveling at the small open shops, the profusion of colorful embroidery, pottery, brass items for sale, the people of different religions and ways of dressing. The road led all the way to the Temple Mount and the Wailing Wall with Arabs walking up the curved walkway to the Dome of the Rock, and Jews bowing and praying before the Wall itself. And behind all of that was the Mount of Olives where Jesus walked and prayed in his time. It was a blessed day!

On my way back I bought a Falafel – chickpeas in a pita bread pocket – and felt on top of the world. There was a sign on the right saying "Hostel", and I went in and found a building from Mameluk Days built 700 years ago with a narrow winding staircase leading to two small rooms with six cots each, each cot to be rented for two shekels per night. I got one cot, which was not too clean looking, and had instead of sheets a kind of horse blanket. So I made a bed for myself using my coat and a t-shirt as a pillow cover. The toilet next door was a hole in the ground. The only source of water for all these people was a small sink (not too clean either). A wonderful adventure, an enchanting day!

I stretched out on my cot in that room with several other women, trying not to move. Very early the next morning, before it became light, there was the call from the Muezzin at the mosque next door, calling the Muslim Believers to prayer - and soon more Muezzins chimed in. The chanting from all over the city was magical, unbelievably beautiful. I was transported to a different time and a different place.

The hostel owner served me a cup of peppermint tea in the tiny sitting room and wished me a good day and mentioned that the Palestinian leadership had proclaimed a day of strike. I did not know what it meant, but when I went down to King David Road it was empty. All stores were closed, not a person in sight! I walked down towards the Temple Mount along the silent street and noticed, on every roof of every building, Israeli soldiers pointing their Uzis into the street. My Uzi guns, all oiled for a fight with Jordan, pointing at whom? There was an ominous feeling of danger and discord. What was going on here?

I walked back to my hostel and there, in the tiny sitting room, I spoke to my very first Palestinian. He was a young man, a student at Birzeit University, speaking fluent English, with a peace medal around his neck and a deep love for his country in his heart. From him I learned about the flip side of the State of Israel: of the people who fled from the Holocaust in Europe only to disenfranchise and dislocate the people living in the country they took over as their own. The first Intifada had started a few months before with youths throwing stones. I asked Khalid, why were they throwing stones? He said, "We are poor. We have no prospects and no hope. We live in deplorable conditions, our land is taken away from us, our olive groves destroyed, and we are treated like second-class citizens in the land of our birth. Having no guns, no ammunition, we throw stones because we somehow must make our presence felt, because the world does not want to see our misery and doesn't care that we, in fact, are forced to pay for the suffering and expulsion of Jews caused by the Nazis in Europe."

They were throwing only stones at the time, hoping for a solution. But nobody listened. Eventually, in desperation, they became what the world calls "terrorists" while they know themselves as "freedom fighters".

Who am I?

We knew in the family that our great grandfather had been an illegitimate child. My grandfather never spoke about it and nobody knew anyone from his branch of the family, but it was known that he carried his mother's name. He was born sometime around 1870 and, as a young man, travelled up the Rhine River, settled in my hometown, and eventually became a prominent business man.

My sister and I fantasized about our forefather. Wasn't the time of my grandfather's birth the time when the French marched back and forth across Germany under Napoleon? Perhaps one of Napoleon's soldiers seduced our great-grandmother, a simple farmer's daughter in a village called Alpenroth in the Westerwald region of Germany. Perhaps she fell in love with a soldier and he marched through and disappeared and she was heart-broken and pined after him all her life? Perhaps he wanted to come back to her and his mother didn't let him? Perhaps ... perhaps? We had a good old time developing scenarios and saw proof of this French connection in the fact that my sister loved French. She spoke it fluently, lived in Paris for a time, and was interested in all things French. There must be a genetic link, we thought.

My father and mother took a vacation and travelled to Alpenroth sometime in the 70's. There they were able to look up the church record where it was recorded that two boys were born on my grandfather's birthday: one had an entry under "Father's Name" with the profession "Day Laborer", and on my grandfather's record was written "Father Unknown". It just must have been a French soldier! But there was nobody left in the town with the family name of Kuenkler, and no Kuenkler farm, and in any case, time went on and obliterated the traces of people and happenings and memories.

On the way back from a vacation in Israel/Palestine in the 90's I spent a few days with my mother in my hometown and accepted an invitation for coffee and cake to an old lady by the name of Ms. Fischmann. Her mother, long since dead, had been Jewish. According to the Nazi Racial Laws, Ms. Fischmann (being a Half-Jew, a "Mischling") was subjected to all sorts of discrimination, including a 1-year stay in a concentration camp towards the end of the War. She was interested in hearing about my Mideast experiences and finally the following conversation ensued:

She: Did you know that my mother came from the same village of Alpenroth as your grandfather?

I: No, I didn't know!

She: And my mother told me that your grandfather, as a boy, herded the cows owned by her family during the summer months.

I: Oh, that is interesting!

She: And my mother told me that your grandfather was the illegitimate son of the local Jewish cattle trader in Alpenroth!

I was speechless! No Napoleonic solder, no heroic stranger, no knight on a white horse, no French blood in us? My mind was working overtime: and I imagined the 19th century village with dirt roads and manure piles, and my grandmother pregnant with a child by a cattle trader! Was she seduced by him? Did she love him? Was she a maid in his household? Was it the cattle trader himself, or his young son, who did the deed? Did she suffer the indignities of an unwed mother? Did he pay the family to keep his name out of the church record?

And then it hit me: my great-grandfather was Jewish! That made my grandfather half-Jewish, my father one quarter-Jewish and me one-eighth Jewish. According to the Racial Laws of the Third Reich both my grandfather and my father would have been disenfranchised and subjected to persecution if Ms. Fischmann's mother, or Ms. Fischmann herself, had ever mentioned a word about this Jewish connection. My family were prominent members of the town, my father was a member of the Party, my mother was well respected, I was a member of the Hitler Youth. All of that would have come to an end, if the Fischmanns had dropped a hint to anyone. To their credit they kept this to themselves, even long after the Nazis had come and gone and a new era had arrived. I suppose their rationale was that it would only cause trouble and do no good to anyone. We children, being one-eighth Jewish, were not considered of mixed blood and might not have been labeled Jewish. But the connection would have touched us anyway.

Is "Jewishness" a religion, a culture, a race, or what? I realize that I cannot call myself Jewish in the religious sense - because Jewishness is handed on by the mother.

It is doubtful that Jews are members of a "Jewish race", as the Nazis assrted in the Nuremberg Racial Laws of 1936. Nobody knows firm rules to evaluate race. In Israel itself you find blue-eyed, fair-skinned, blond children playing next to brown-eyed, brown-skinned, dark-haired children, all of Middle-Eastern origin. There are very learned books by academic experts who deal with these issues of race. I defer to them and can only state that I believe there is only one race, and that is: the human race.

Culture, however, may be the defining aspect – a Jewish viewpoint or worldview developed over centuries, based on belief systems, art, music, history, group living. Even my friends at the Kibbutz called themselves Jewish, even though some of them were atheists ("I don't think there is a God. If there were one - how could he have permitted the Holocaust?") And on the Kibbutz there was no synagogue, no religious service, very little in the way of holiday celebrations. After all, kibbutzniks were die-hard Socialists. But if asked them who they were: they said they were Jewish, and proud of it. The common history draws them to Jewishness.

But now I know that I am part Jewish, however that may be defined! I remember the day in Jerusalem when I sat an entire day on the plaza facing the Wailing Wall and the Dome of the Rock and the Mount of Olives and was transfixed by something I could not understand. It was as if something called me bit I did not know what. But I now know that one of my ancestors in the distant past was led by Moses from Egypt: waited at the foot of Mt. Sinai for him to come back from the mountain top; settled in the Palestinian heartland; might well have worshipped near the very spot I was sitting, was dispersed by the Romans, travelled to Europe, made a life in a small village called Alpenroth, met my great grandmother Annemarie and produced my grandfather. Two generations later, a girl named Inge was born. All these strands, connecting people all over the world, connected with other strands, produced a child who hated Jews with a vengeance who eventually found out that she was only hating her own essence.

Israel and Palestine

For the rest of my stay in Israel I travelled by bus and train, hitchhiked when necessary, stayed in Acco, Haifa, Old Jerusalem and Eilat in youth hostels, visited archeological sites and spoke to people of all walks of life. One day, in Galilee, I walked off the road and discovered ruins of a crusader castle in a steep ravine. Another day I roamed over the hills bordering on Lebanon. There I was invited to a Palestinian's house and offered a place on the floor of the living room - which was covered with quilts at night to give the entire family a place to sleep. The next evening I found myself on a meadow at sundown in the middle of a herd of sheep, and that's where I spent the night.

Several days were spent at a Kibbutz near the Dead Sea. I swam in the salty water and plastered myself with the black mud promising healing properties. I visited Sodom and Gomorrah and the salt column of Lot's wife, as well as the caves of Qumran where, in the 40's, bible fragments were found in clay containers. I explored the oasis of Jericho, one of the oldest towns in the history of mankind. On another day I climbed Masada in searing heat, noting the ancient outline of a Roman camp in the valley, and seeing the soldiers building a ramp on the side of the mountain, ready for the final conquest. I imagined the desperate resolve of the inhabitants who, in the face of certain death at the hands of the conquerors, decided to take their own lives instead. It reminded me of the time when I was twelve and the victors, American troops, were closing in on my hometown under cover of exploding grenades and bombs. My girlfriend's father could not bear the thought of being conquered by the enemy – so he shot his entire family and then killed himself.

At one point I rented a car and drove through the West Bank and the Gaza Strip with a friend, Khalid, the 25-year old Palestinian who wore a peace medal around his neck and whom I had met in the Arab youth hostel in the old city of Jerusalem. He took me to see friends and relatives in villages and refugee camps and changed my view of the situation in a profound way. After having lived with Israelis and having listened to their narratives for months, I now came to know Palestinians and listened to their stories.

Palestinian villages and homes are poor and worn down. In many homes quilts are spread on the floor of the living room at night to give a sleeping space to extended families.

Cooking is often done on the outside cement patio on a little gas burner. Wash is done there, too, and clothes hang on the roof to dry. Bathrooms are frequently hole-in-the-ground affairs with a pitcher of water next to it, and there is a sink in the living area to wash up before meals. But guests are welcomed with such warmth and kindness that one forgets the poor surroundings. We were invited to stay overnight at several homes and slept with everybody else on the living room floor. Long hours were spent talking and listening to our hosts. Sometimes I would sit among the simplicity of their homes and remember with a feeling of guilt the riches, the property, the abundance, the space, the privacy, the things my home in the United States provided for me.

And so I learned about the framework of my newfound friends' lives: the difficulty of finding work, the hardship of getting to work or school through checkpoints and road closings, the hopelessness and despair underlying every new day, the effort it takes to find and pay for food, to take the occupiers' insults, the constant effort to affirm one's value while being treated as a second-class citizen. It all started with the occupation of the land by the State of Israel and the building of Jewish settlements on almost every hilltop. These were white gleaming buildings with community centers and swimming pools and green lawns, on land taken away from the Palestinians, land that had nurtured their olive groves and fields for centuries. 280,000 settlers live in the West Bank, and there are 200,000 Jews in Arab East Jerusalem. These settlements are connected with special access roads which Palestinians are not allowed to use and which also separate them from their land. A Palestinian may not build a house for his family without permits, and permits are not given. If he adds to his house, the soldiers will come and tear it down, sometimes repeatedly. High walls run along the inside of large sections of the border. Water is pumped first to the settlements, leaving the Palestinians only a few hours of water access per day. Going anywhere means standing for hours at checkpoints. Medical care is minimal, and people sometimes die in ambulances because the army won't open the checkpoint to let them through. Palestinian produce has to wait long hours in trucks before it is allowed across the border, and often rots in the fields because no workers can get through checkpoints. Palestinian life is so difficult. It is obvious that Israeli power is overwhelming and insurmountable at this time. Anger grows with the Palestinian sense of helplessness. Israelis speak about the possibility of peace, with the subtext "without giving up the settlements". Palestinians say they want peace with justice (namely the return of their land) because for them there is no peace possible without justice.

What is my country's involvement in this tragedy? Israel is the highest recipient of US Foreign Aid: $15 million/day including gifts & loans (IfAmericansKnew.org) and it is the only recipient of US aid not held accountable for how that aid is spent. This, despite having violated more UN Resolutions than Iraq, Iran, or any other country in the UN.

"The moral arc of the universe is long, but it bends toward justice." – Martin Luther King Jr.

Hebron

In 1995 I learned about an organization leading delegations into Israel/Palestine with the intention of teaching participants to listen to the narrative of both sides of the conflict, in order to understand their experiences and the reasons for their actions. It was during this time that I became fascinated by paradigms, belief systems and worldviews. Had I not once followed the dictates of the Nazi worldview without question? Hadn't I, in time, been able to question that worldview and select a more fitting, more just one? I joined one of the delegations to Israel/Palestine arranged by The Mideast Citizens Diplomacy Organization and was thrown into a world of conflicting convictions treasured by two groups, both convinced that the land under their feet was theirs.

The Organization had arranged for interviews with many officials in the Israeli government, different Kibbutz organizations, and liaison officers with the Israeli Defense Forces in the Occupied Territories, as well as with officials in Arafat's Fatah government and ordinary people on both sides. We spent several weeks in the West Bank and the Gaza strip, and a week in Hebron where we lived with Palestinian families and experienced their daily struggles first hand.

If ever there was a heart-breaking town, it is Hebron. 4000 years ago, Abraham moved north with his wife Sarah and his flock to Canaan, and as the Bible states in Genesis, God promised the land to him and his offspring. Two sons were born to Abraham: Ishmael, the son of a maid servant and himself the father of Arab tribes, and later Isaac, the son of Abraham's wife Sarah who became pregnant late in life. Isaac is considered the forefather of the Jewish population. Abraham treated his sons differently, but both of them came together in peace to bury Abraham next to his wife Sarah, in the cave he had purchased for 400 shekels years before.

Today 450 Israeli settlers, protected by about 4,000 Israeli soldiers, are living within the city limits of Hebron in the midst of approximately 180,000 Palestinians. My delegation visited a private home and spoke to four Israeli settler women, learning first-hand of their determination to regain Hebron, which they consider theirs by right, because the

Bible says God had given it to them. It is often mentioned that in 1935 Arabs killed 56 Jews and for a few years ended the Jewish presence in Hebron. It is not mentioned often, however, that during that time Arab neighbors sheltered hundreds of their Jewish neighbors and brought them to safety. Today the Hebron settlers are by far the most violent settlers in Palestine, rampaging regularly through Palestinian areas and homes and committing frequent and horrific abuses of defenseless Palestinians. A few years ago a Jewish Medical Doctor, originally from Brooklyn, entered the mosque and shot 28 Palestinians during Friday prayer. International peacekeepers, Israeli and Palestinian human rights organizations, and even Israeli soldiers, are helpless in the face of their onslaught and determination. Even the settlers' children are encouraged to harass and hurt Palestinian adults and school children. Palestinians living or working near the settlement have abandoned their homes and businesses, turning the area into a ghost town. We heard terrible and heart-breaking reports which prompting the then Prime Minister Olmert to state in December 2008 during the weekly cabinet meeting: "We are the children of a people whose historic ethos is built on the memory of pogroms. The sight of Jews firing at innocent Palestinians has no other name than pogrom. I am ashamed that Jews could do such a thing."

For me, Hebron closed the circle between my upbringing as an indoctrinated Nazi child who was taught to hate Jews, and the upbringing of Zionist settlers and their children who hate, abuse and obstruct Palestinians. What is the difference between an unrepentant fascist, who wants Germany occupied only by members of his own race, caring nothing about anybody else, and an equally unrepentant Zionists who wants only what is good for the Jewish settlers in the land of Israel? The Jewish Holocaust perpetrated by Germans eliminated the "undesirables" and was used as justification for the Zionist purpose. But the settlers are organizing their very own Palestinian "Kristallnacht" right now and would not shrink to organize a Palestinian "Holocaust" if it cleared Zion (without media observation) for occupation by Jews alone.

The Israeli government itself is perpetuating this hard-line treatment of the Palestinians. In 2009 home-made rockets without explosives were lobbed across the border into Israeli border towns, killing three Israelis (four more were killed by "friendly fire"). According to B'Tselem, the Israeli Human Rights Organization, the extensive retaliation with F-22 bombers, tanks and pin-point bombing of the Gaza towns, laid large areas to waste, killed 1,387 Palestinians (mostly civilians), destroyed 20,000 buildings and caused massive damage, leading to numerous allegations of war crimes. The Red Cross reported that medical care was denied to the wounded and ambulances were prevented from reaching their destinations. The United Nations human rights investigator for the Palestinian territories, Richard Falk, issued a report declaring that Israel's siege of Gaza "would seem to constitute a war crime of the gravest magnitude under international law." It described the Israeli campaign as a "massive assault on a densely populated urbanized setting" that subjected civilians to "an inhumane form of warfare that kills, maims and inflicts mental harm."

Falk listed war crimes such as the "targeting of schools, mosques and ambulances" and the use of white phosphorus shells in densely populated neighborhoods. The war on Gaza was not legally justified and could constitute a "crime against peace," he argued. This was also the principal charge against the Nazi leaders tried at Nuremberg.

■■

It is always of a surprise to me to see that a people that suffered so much under a cruel system, as the Jews did during the Holocaust, can keep the memory of that Holocaust alive while visiting a similar kind of devastation on another people. I know that not enough Germans stood up when the Nazis rounded up their neighbors and sent them to concentration camps, and the mark will be on them forever. There are many Jewish peace activists in Israel, but where was the Israeli conscience when this Gaza attack took place?

Dr. Eyad Sarraj, the President of the Gaza Mental Health Commission, gave a very compassionate explanation of that silence. He said that the wanton killing of women and children during the 22-day attack on Gaza reflected Israel's systematic de-humanization of the Palestinian "other". He traced the origins of this destructive syndrome back to the historical vulnerability and outcast status of Jews themselves, which culminated in the Holocaust. If unresolved and untreated, these anxieties result in turning former victims into future perpetrators. He observed that Israeli discourse towards Palestinians directly borrows the language of genocidal contempt that paved the way to the Final Solution (Dr. Sarraj statement before Judge Richard Goldstone at the UN War Crimes Commission investigating the 2008/2009 Israeli assault on Gaza).

God, the God I am not so sure even exists, every once in a while, should find somebody who will say "Enough!."

Mt. Sinai

The most deeply felt spiritual experience during my travels through Israel/Palestine was the climb to Mount Sinai before sunrise. I had booked a land rover trip down into the Egyptian Sinai Peninsula with a guide called Yossi who, with his curly hair and sandals, looked like one of the old Israelites himself. He showed us Wadi Paran which is one of the main Bedouin routes through the desert, took us to Bedouin camps, and old settlements on mountain tops and near water holes. We finally arrived in a Bedouin camp near St. Katherine, the monastery at the foot of Mount Sinai, where we all slept next to each other on a platform covered with quilts. Before bedtime we sat around outside under a sky ablaze with stars, incredibly grateful about this experience.

The next morning at 3 am Yossi woke us up, offered us a cup of tea and some pita bread, and we were on our way to the top of the mountain to see the sun come up. It was apparent to me very soon that, as the oldest person in the group, I could not keep up with the others. Yossi and I agreed that they all would go ahead and I would follow at my own pace. They disappeared around the bend and I found myself utterly alone on the mountain path on a stony outcropping in a completely silent world. There was no sound, no sound at all. Utter silence reigned. Slowly it got lighter, the sky became dark grey and then light grey, and finally revealed the waves of hills receding into the distance. Then the sun came over the horizon, first as a little point, then bigger and bigger and blood red, until the light flooded the world in a brilliant abundance of luminosity. I sat on a boulder and drank in the indescribable wonder of life, of pulsating, radiating power – existing existed from time immemorial, through the days of the earliest humans, whether seen or not, whether appreciated or not, whether viewed by believers or humans like me who have such trouble with religion or God or faith. For the rest of my life, whenever doubt appears, I remember Mount Sinai as proof of the power of nature which will make death, my Death, when it comes, an ecstatic passage into the blood-red substance of the light of the sun.

Then a camel appeared on the path, led by a camel driver who had taken a visitor up to the mountain before and was coming down empty. He was a middle aged man, a Bedouin, very friendly. He sat down next to me to smoke a cigarette and we chatted for a while in English, two strangers with worlds separating us. Finally he offered me a ride on his camel down the mountain to the gate of St. Katherine Monastery, where I joined up with my group later that morning. And so I rode from the height of ecstasy back into my daily life on the back of a swaying, lumbering, smelly camel.

Jerusalem

At the end of my 6-months stay in the Mideast in 1988, I had seen the glory and beauty of Israel and the degradation and despair of the Palestinian population within Israel and the Territories. It seemed to me then, to my great sadness, that the overwhelming Israeli power and determination to assure its continued dominance would not allow a Palestinian State next to it. Only its dissolution or the formation of a single state for Jews and Arabs alike would guarantee a peaceful rearrangement of the Mideast situation. If you want peace, you must work for justice!

This is what I wrote about the last day of my stay:

"Zionism did pursue its dreams of a Jewish homeland in Palestine without recognizing that Palestine is also the homeland for another people. The Arabs (Christian or

Moslem) who have lived there for hundreds of years, perhaps thousands of years, must (even if diluted and changed) also be the descendants of the Philistines and other Semitic tribes who occupied this sliver of land.

Was Zionism built on the wrong premise? Yes, I believe it was. But extenuating circumstances can be found in the fact that it arose during the time of conquest of less developed lands, of colonial expansion, or the glorious moves into new territories. If at all, the Zionists had more right to their conquest than others because they did not want to subjugate and suppress for their own material gain. Rather they wanted to find a homeland after centuries of persecution, in which almost all countries in the world had taken part. Nobody who has studied the holocaust can deny the crying and pressing need to find a haven, a harbor, a refuge for the victims of anti-Semitism. Nobody can deny them the right to fight for a place where "the word Jew is not considered an insult".

After living on a kibbutz and on an army base and staying in youth hostels during my travels, for the last night I rented a room at the Intercontinental Hotel on the Mount of Olives in Jerusalem. My room overlooked the Old City of Jerusalem, the Temple Mount with the golden Dome of the Rock and the adjacent City of David, and to the left I could see

Bethlehem in the distance. Further to the right lay the ancient city of Jericho. I sat at the window from noon of one day to noon of the next, through dusk and night and dawn, while reading the Old Testament from cover to cover and feasting my eyes on this incomparable sight. Many of the events described in the bible happened right there in front of me. The history of Israel is one of epic proportions. Power and conquests, weakness and loss, constant growth and decay, ever-present change symbolizes the history of this land. Peace only reigned for short periods of time. Then the balance of power shifted and internal or external pressure led to a new political arrangement: to a (in the final analysis) temporary solution. The Old City of Jerusalem before my window was conquered 38 times through history, and every conquest was devastating for the residents, inconceivable in its implications. Is it possible that, seen in the grand sweep of history, the Jewish State of Israel is only another episode like many others before? Reading, as I did, of the biblical events of 4000 years and seeing before me the very places where they occurred, I could not help but see the current existence of Israel as an episode, a passing phase, one more heartbreaking historical event like so many before, only one event in a chain of events reaching from the distant past into the future. The power in Israel has already begun to shift. Desperate measures can stem the tide of change, but cannot stop it. Time will roll on and somehow, in some fashion, life will go on and arrange itself until that arrangement in turn will be put to the test. Change, like life and death, growth and decay, is the only constant in history."

(Master Thesis, 1990)

Trying to find an answer

Over the years I took many workshops and college courses as part of a life-long process of learning beginning on that fateful day when, as a child, I saw concentration camp survivors stumble along the road. One of the first was the Compassionate Listening Project which "teaches heart-based skills to create powerful cultures of peace in our families, communities, in the workplace, and in the world". The idea is to listen to the narrative of a person without preconceived notions or convictions and understand the other from the bottom of one's being. The organization has been very successful in training many people in the development of compassion. It is not meant to provide answers, but to be healing by engaging the participants in seeing the humanity of the others, even when they disagree. It is just that I feel that developing compassion and understanding must ultimately lead to a conclusion and must make a jump from the heart to some kind of ethical action.

In 2005 my Alma Mater, Queens College, introduced a history course I was able to audit as a senior alumni. It was conducted by a Professor who saw increasing numbers of Muslims study alongside Jews and was interested in involving young people from both groups in a dialogue concerning the Israeli/Palestinian conflict. The result was extremely interesting and greatly influenced many, if not all, of the participants.

Queens is a true melting pot. 170 nationalities live here, and the children of many of them find their way to Queens College. The class consisted of retired community residents, social studies teachers and principals and Queens College students, from Muslims activist to Orthodox Jews and Christians. We studied texts, read newspaper articles, and listened to guest speakers from both sides of the divide, in addition to US government officials. We had lively discussions and were guided by the Professor, who had extensive experience with roundtable talks with Palestinians and Israelis and himself had participated in peace negotiations. The High School teachers intended to learn how to help their own students carry on a political debate at home and to understand some of the motivations driving the other side. A number of the seniors were holocaust survivors. And there I was: the lone German with her experience as a Nazi child and her realization of the injustice done to the Jews and others. Sometimes it is hard for me to stand up and talk about my path, but I also feel that it is important for others to recognize that there is salvation in admitting the error in following a worldview neglecting humanitarian concern for the life of others. To me it seems obvious that this realization would lead to a recognition of the right to justice and equality for both sides in the Israeli/Palestinian conflict, at least as a basic concept. But that is not always the case.

The Professor's idea was to have his students explore their own feelings about the conflict and then use the rest of the semester to step into the other side's shoes and try to understand and present that viewpoint. A lot of learning took place, reason was applied, some understanding was gained, perspectives were adjusted, but nobody switched his position. I know only too well how deep the indoctrination goes (all childhood learning is indoctrination) and how difficult it is to go into unchartered waters and let go of the basic assumptions underlying the worldview of an entire people. We need more courses like this one, letting students analyze their own feelings and measure them against the situation "on the ground".

The workshop I preferred above all others was the Grassroots Advocacy Training conducted by Interfaith Peace-Builders in Washington, D.C. Interfaith Peace-Builders works with the U.S. Campaign to End the Israeli Occupation and dozens of other U.S., Israeli and Palestinian peace organizations. As it turns out, there are many peace activist groups in Israel and the U.S., with many different approaches, but not always sufficiently covered in the media. After the workshop almost 200 participants from almost every state in the Union visited their Congressmen at the Capitol to lobby for or encourage legislation favorable to peace.

The workshop itself answered many questions for me. The most important was how I can reconcile my German guilt and painful memorirswith necessary action. Too often my accent led to the immediate conviction that, as a German, I had to be anti-Semitic. It also clarified for me how I can express my love for Israel and the Israelis, my best wishes for their happiness in their homeland, with the fervent desire to make sure that the Palestinians also experience justice and peace. Given the large number of peace-building organizations, I realize I am not alone.

The most valuable advice given was to always keep in mind the difference between Jews, Israelis, and Zionists.

To be Jewish is to belong to the Jewish faith or blood-line. To be Israeli is to have citizenship from the state of Israel. Zionism is a political movement supporting the Jewish state in historic Palestine, often unconditionally. There can be overlap between the categories, but they are *not* the same thing. There are Jews who are not Israeli, Israelis who are not Jewish, Jews who are anti-Zionist, and Zionists who are not Jewish (like Christian Zionists).

There are different areas one may focus on in working for Israeli/Palestinian justice, not all of them suitable for everybody. Israel's accountability is one, US involvement another, but mine is the humanitarian aspect. The holocaust, the defining event in my own life, was of humanitarian importance and I feel able to extend my concerns for the fate of Jews and other suppressed minorities to the fate of Palestinians. There is not much I can do (I have bum knees and can't walk well), but I can write and talk to people and keep the fire for justice alive. And I can always state with conviction that the horrors exemplified by the Holocaust must never again happen to people of any religious, racial, ethnic or national origin.

Looking back at what really mattered

The sun is almost down. I have tried to look at different aspects of my life – by no means all, but the ones that were very important to me. From this vantage point I can look back and see the wavering will, the diffused focus, the lack of courage, the constant struggle for truth, the wrong decisions – but time has gone by and nothing can be changed now.

The important people in my life, all - like me - flawed but important nevertheless, were my mother; my sister Maddalena; my husband Helmut (who promised to grow old with me and then died way too early); my children Martina, Stefanie and Chris, who carry on my and Helmut's spirit; and my friend George, the person who understood that I am a bird and must fly sometimes, and offered himself as the rock I can land on when I come back. I thank all of them for their contribution to my life.

Then there is my little house in the country: white, with large windows, holding my stained glass panels through which the sun shines. It is the first place that is wholly mine and occupied only by me. It was built on the flank of the Taconic mountain range and offers views of the wide sky, the stars and, every four weeks, the magnificent full moon.

And there is the Roe-Jan Library in Hillsdale, NY: a treasure of a place, which gave me much pleasure and abundant opportunities to be useful. It also gave me a place to conduct meetings of the Socrates Café philosophical discussion group, examining issues of ethics and conversing with like-minded people. Philosophy is my favorite subject and I sometimes drive people to distraction because I see ethical angles behind every event.

The questions I had always been most interested in, though, were those dealing with personal ethics. To my dismay they often clash with ethics involving society. The focus of personal ethics is unselfishness; whereas the highest moral ideal of political groups is justice. Greed and power are hindrances to both personal and political ethics, and the complexity of some situations requires detailed examination of their components. For instance, what events would be necessary to shift Israel's power sufficiently to allow the establishment of an equitable and just state for Palestinians? What must happen before a power-wielding entity will give up some power to allow the other side to live with dignity? I believe that the highest moral insights and achievements of the individual conscience are both relevant and necessary to the life of society, as stars to steer our ships by, even though we have to struggle to reconcile ethics and politics.

On the first day of my Existentialism class at Queens College I came across Bertrand Russell's essay "A Free Man's Worship". It struck me as so existentially "me" that I carried it around with me for 35 years, reading and examining it again and again since that day, and it is still the truest and clearest expression of what I hold dear. Here is an excerpt:

"The life of Man is a long march through the night, surrounded by invisible forces, tortured by weariness and pain, towards a goal that few can hope to reach, and where none may tarry long. One by one, as they march, our comrades vanish from our sight, seized by the silent orders of omnipotent Death. Very brief is the time in which we can help them, in which their happiness or misery is decided. Be it ours to shed sunshine on their path, to lighten their sorrows by the balm of sympathy, to give them the pure joy of a never-tiring affection, to strengthen failing courage, to instill faith in hours of despair. Let us not weigh in grudging scales their merits and demerits, but let us think only of their need -- of the sorrows, the difficulties, perhaps the blindnesses, that make the misery of their lives; let us remember that they are fellow-sufferers in the same darkness, actors in the same tragedy with ourselves. And so, when their day is over, when their good and their evil have become eternal by the immortality of the past, be it ours to feel that, where they suffered, where they failed, no deed of ours was the cause; but wherever a spark of the divine fire kindled in their hearts, we were ready with encouragement, with sympathy, with brave words in which high courage glowed."[1]

---

[1] www.philosophicalsociety.com

Biography

Inge Etzbach was born in Germany in 1932, and because of her experiences during the War and the Hitler years came to feel a deep connection with Israel and Palestine. Questions of ethics and morality are of great interest to her and color other issues dealing with life and death and the overriding importance of compassion.

When her youngest child started school, Inge entered Queens College and studied Philosophy, graduating in 1985 with a B.A. in Philosophy and in 1991 with a M.A. in Political Science. She is also an ordained Interfaith Minister. In 1987 she spent several months in Israel, working in a kibbutz and as a volunteer in the Israeli Army. Over the next few years she participated in several Peace-Building Delegations which interacted with Israeli and Palestinian officials and ordinary citizens in Israel and the West Bank, participated in Mideast Workshops and also travelled in the area on her own.

She has three grown children and lives in New York City and Copake Falls, NY

Reference

Baltzer, Anna – Witness in Palestine

- Life in Occupied Palestine, DVD

- www.annainthemiddleeast.com-

Russell, Bertrand – A Free Man's Worship

Niebuhr, Reinhold – Moral Man & Immoral Society

Interfaith Peace-Builders – www.ifpb.org

The US Campaign to End the Israeli Occupation – www.endtheoccupation.org

The American-Arab Anti-Discrimination Committee - www.adc.org

The Israeli Committee Against House Demolitions – USA – www.icahdusa.org

The Middle East Research and Information Project – www.merip.org

Progressive Democrats of America – www.pdamerica.org

The Washington Peace Center – www.washingtonpeacecenter.org

Made in the USA
Charleston, SC
10 April 2010